Haunting Histories

Plays by Steve Barlow
and Steve Skidmore

Illustrated by Chris Jevons

Pearson Australia
(a division of Pearson Australia Group Pty Ltd)
707 Collins Street, Melbourne, Victoria 3008
PO Box 23360, Melbourne, Victoria 8012
www.pearson.com.au

Text by Steve Barlow and Steve Skidmore
Illustrated by Chris Jevons
Designed by Sara Rafferty

First published 2013 by Pearson Education Limited.
This edition first published 2016 by Pearson Australia Group Pty Ltd by arrangement with Pearson Education Limited.

2019 2018 2017 2016
10 9 8 7 6 5 4 3 2 1

ISBN 978 1 4886 1242 8

Pearson Australia Group Pty Ltd ABN 40 004 245 943

Printed in Australia by SOS Print+Media Group

Off to the Tower!

Characters

Outside the Tower of London

Beefeater: Good morning, everyone. Welcome to the Tower of London.

Emma: I've got a bad feeling about this, Mia.

Mia: Me too, Emma. It's going to be soooo boring!

Raj: Why couldn't we have gone to Mega World Theme Park? They have great rides.

Katy: Mrs Smith said it wasn't educational, Raj. We wouldn't learn anything.

Josh: Well, I don't learn anything from Mrs Smith ...

Emma: Josh, you don't learn anything from anyone!

Beefeater: All right, settle down, please. I am a Yeoman warder.

Mia: Yo, man!

Beefeater: I am also known as a Beefeater.

Raj: I couldn't be a Beefeater – I'm vegetarian!

Emma: Good one, Raj!

Beefeater: Oh yes, very funny, I'm sure. Now, the Tower of London was built nearly a thousand years ago.

Katy: I wish I'd been born a thousand years ago.

Josh: Why?

Katy: Just think of all the history I wouldn't have had to learn ...

Beefeater: It was built by William the Conqueror. Who knows why 1066 is important?

Emma: Is it because it was William the Conqueror's phone number?

Beefeater: No! 1066 was the year William conquered the Saxons. William was a Norman.

Raj: I thought you said he was a William. How can he be called Norman?

Beefeater: William was his name, but he was a Norman because ...

Mia: Look, Mr Beefeater, history is boring ...

Beefeater: Of course it isn't. There are lots of exciting things here ...

Emma: Really? What kinds of things?

Beefeater: Like ghosts for example. Legend has it that several ghosts haunt the Tower. For instance, Sir Walter Raleigh.

Josh: Didn't he invent the potato?

Beefeater: Well, he **brought** potatoes back from America ...

Katy: Why didn't he just buy them from the supermarket like everyone else?

Beefeater: Then there was Guy Fawkes. He was arrested for trying to blow up the Houses of Parliament on the 5th of November and taken straight to prison.

Raj: Oh, that's a shame. He must have missed bonfire night.

Beefeater: But there wouldn't have **been** a bonfire night unless ... Oh, never mind!

Mia: When do these ghosts appear?

Katy: Just before someone screams!

Mia: That is **so** pathetic!

Raj: Hey, what's a ghost's favourite game?

Josh: I don't know, what **is** a ghost's favourite game?

Raj: Hide and shriek!

Beefeater: I wish I could hide you lot! If I may continue … here on Tower Green, two of Henry the Eighth's wives had their heads chopped off.

Mia: Henry the Eighth – didn't he discover fractions?

Josh: Funny joke, Mia. Even **I** know Henry the Eighth was famous for having six wives … or was it Henry the Sixth who had eight wives?

Katy: Do you know why Henry the Eighth had so many wives?

Emma: No idea.

Katy: Because he liked to chop and change!

Raj: That's terrible!

Beefeater: The two queens executed by Henry were Anne Boleyn and Catherine Howard.

Josh: I know a fact about Anne Boleyn.

Emma: No way, Josh!

Josh: I do. Anne Boleyn never walked anywhere – she was always running.

Raj: Why was she always running?

Josh: Because she wanted to get ahead ... Get a head. Get it?

Mia: I know something else about Anne Boleyn. She invented a very popular sport.

Emma: A sport?

Katy: Did she?

Mia: Of course. Haven't you heard of Ten-Pin Boleyn?

Katy: That's terrible!

Beefeater: To get back to my story. Does anyone know when Anne Boleyn died?

Josh: When they chopped her head off!

Beefeater: No! I meant when was she executed?

The kids mumble and shake their heads.

Beefeater: Any ideas? All right, I'll tell you. It was 1536.

Raj looks at his watch.

Raj: Oh, we've just missed it. It's four o'clock now!

Beefeater: I meant the **year** 1536. Don't they teach you anything at school?

Josh: Mrs Smith doesn't.

Katy: She only tells us about boring things like dates and battles, not beheadings and ghosts.

Mia: Does Henry the Eighth's ghost walk around here?

Beefeater: No. He was buried at Windsor Castle.

Emma: Why was he buried at Windsor Castle?

Katy: Because he was dead! Duh!

Beefeater: I don't know why I'm wasting my breath asking you this, but does anyone know when Henry died?

Josh: A few days before they buried him.

Beefeater: Not another terrible joke! Don't you take anything seriously?

Raj: **Seriously?** How can we take anything seriously when you keep telling us stories about ghosts?

Emma: That's right. Ghosts! Hah! You're just trying to scare us!

Mia: Yeah! Ghosts aren't real!

Josh: Even I know that!

Beefeater: Oh, but they are ...

Katy: Really? Have you seen one?

Beefeater: Oh yes. Every time I look in a mirror ... Goodbye!

The Beefeater vanishes into thin air.

Kids: **ARRGGHHHHH!**

We Are Not Amused!

Characters

Inside Buckingham Palace

Emma: Honestly, why do you guys always need to go to the toilet just when the coach is about to leave? We're going to be late.

Mia: Yes – Mrs Smith'll be really cross if she has to come looking for us.

Victoria: Ooooooh!

Katy: What was that?

Raj: What was what?

Emma: You know, that ...

Victoria: Oooooh ...!

Emma: ... noise.

Josh: There it is again!

Emma: I thought everyone had been to the toilet ...

Raj: It's not us!

Mia: It's coming from the throne, through there.

Victoria: Oooooh!

Katy: Oo-er!

Mia: It's a ghost!

Emma: How do you know?

Mia: It's the way you can see right through her. It's a dead giveaway.

Raj: But whose ghost is it?

Victoria: We are the ghost of Queen Victoria.

Josh: Wh-a-a-at are you doing here?

Victoria: What do you mean, what are we doing here? We live here! What are **you** doing here?

Emma: We're on a school trip.

Victoria: Well, you should have gone home ages ago. The palace is closed!

Emma: I told you we didn't have time to go to the toilet …

Raj: Wow – is that really Queen Victoria? That's amazing. She had the longest reign in history.

Josh: She must have got very wet.

Raj: That's 'reign' as in ruling, not 'rain' as in pouring, Josh!

Katy: Well, I don't care if you **are** Queen Victoria. It was mean of you to try to scare us.

Victoria: Who was trying to scare you?

Mia: You were! All that "Oooooh!" business.

Victoria: We were not trying to scare you, foolish child! We were groaning.

Raj: Why?

Victoria: Because it's no fun being a ghost. One can't even have a chat with a living person unless they speak first.

Emma: Why's that?

Victoria: We're not allowed to spook till we're spoken to. Being dead is dead boring! We are not amused!

Josh: Why does she keep saying "we" this and "we" that?

Emma: All Royals do that. It's called the "Royal We".

Josh: The "Royal We", eh? Sounds like somebody else needs the toilet ...

Mia: No, you noodle ...

Raj: Hey, I've got an idea – we could try to cheer you up!

Katy: How?

Josh: I've got some card tricks ...

Emma: Oh, no, Josh.

Mia: We've seen your card tricks.

Josh: Come on, give me a chance. Here, your majesty. Take a card – any card. Put it back on top of the pack. I will now tell you which card you have chosen ...

Mia: Shouldn't she have put it back face **down**?

Josh: Oh, I've tried it that way. It doesn't work.

Katy: Rubbish!

Victoria: We are **still** not amused.

Josh: At least my tricks always work. My success rate is a hundred percent.

Emma: But your entertainment value is nil.

Raj: I could do a rap. Like, "I just met Queen Victoria, and ..."

Mia: Why have you stopped?

Raj: I can't think of anything that rhymes with "Victoria".

Katy: How about, "I know you did, I saw ya!"

Josh: "Now I don't want to bore ya ..."

Mia: "... Victoria, I adore ya!"

Raj: Now you're just being silly.

Emma: We could try a few jokes.

Raj: Yeah, good idea. Like, how do you stop fish from smelling?

Katy: I don't know.

Raj: Cut off their noses!

Emma: She's not going to laugh at that joke – it's older than she is!

Mia: All right, try this one. What's brown and sticky?

Josh: I don't know.

Mia: A stick.

Victoria: We are **definitely** not amused!

Katy: No wonder – that was pathetic!

Josh: Go on, then, you do one.

Katy: Where do you take a whale to find out how heavy it is? A whale-weigh station!

Emma: What time is it when an elephant sits on your fence? Time to get a new one!

Josh: Here, I've got a good one. What goes "zzub zzub"?

Mia: I don't know.

Josh: A bee flying backwards.

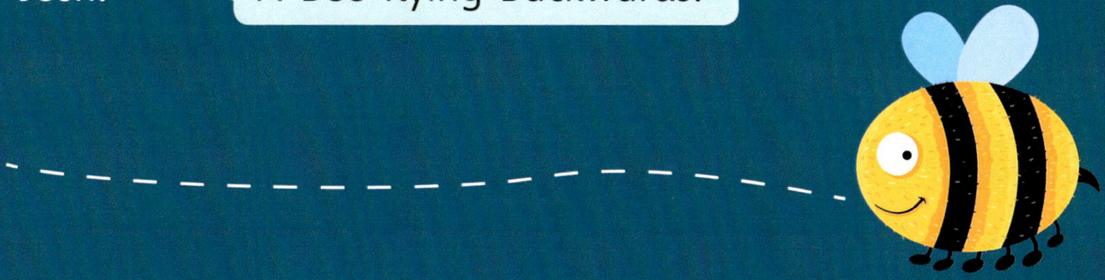

Mia: I don't get it.

Victoria: **We** get it. But we are **absolutely** not amused!

Raj: Goodness – there's no pleasing some people. I'm off!

Emma: Where are you going, Raj?

Katy: Watch out for that lump in the rug!

Raj: Aaaarrgh!

Emma: He's slipped up!

Mia: Enjoy your trip!

Josh: Oh, look where he's fallen – right into that plant over there.

Raj: I wondered why the plant pot was getting bigger – then it hit me. Ow!

Josh: Oh no! Mind that suit of armour.

Raj: Aaarrgh!

Katy: He's dropped a clanger!

Mia: Be careful of the drapes, Raj! Oh dear – down they come!

Emma: Looks like it's curtains for him. Ha, ha!

Raj: It's not funny!

Katy: Hey – look at Queen Victoria!

Mia: She's smiling ...

Emma: ... she's chuckling ...

Josh: ... she's laughing!

Victoria: Now, we **are** amused!